FOLLOW THOSE ZEBRAS

SOLVING A MIGRATION MYSTERY

SANDRA MARKLE

M MILLBROOK PRESS
MINNEAPOLIS

**FOR PENNY SWEENEY AND THE CHILDREN OF
WILLOW FIELD ELEMENTARY IN LIVERPOOL, NEW YORK**

The author would like to thank the following people for sharing their enthusiasm and expertise: Dr. Chloe Bracis, Senckenberg Biodiversity and Climate Research Centre & Goethe University, Frankfurt, Germany; Dr. Hattie Bartlam-Brooks, Botswana Herbivore Research, Botswana & Royal Veterinary College, London; Dr. Robin Naidoo, Conservation Science Program, World Wildlife Fund-US, Washington, DC; and Robert Sutcliffe, Elephants Without Borders, Botswana. And a special thank-you to Skip Jeffery for his loving support during the creative process.

Millbrook Press™
An imprint of Lerner Publishing Group, Inc.
241 First Avenue North
Minneapolis, MN 55401 USA

For reading levels and more information, look up this title at www.lernerbooks.com.

Main body text set in Charter ITC Std.
Typeface provided by International Typeface Corporation.

Library of Congress Cataloging-in-Publication Data

Names: Markle, Sandra, author.
Title: Follow those zebras! : solving a migration mystery / by Sandra Markle.
Description: Minneapolis : Millbrook Press, [2020] | Series: Sandra Markle's science discoveries | Includes bibliographical references and index. | Audience: Age 8–12. | Audience: Grade 4 to 6.
Identifiers: LCCN 2019022077 (print) | LCCN 2019022316 (ebook) | ISBN 9781541538375 (lb : alk. paper)
Subjects: LCSH: Zebras—Migration—Namibia—Juvenile literature.
Classification: LCC QL737.U62 M3727 2020 (print) | LCC QL737.U62 (ebook) | DDC 599.665/71568—dc23

LC record available at https://lccn.loc.gov/2019022077
LC ebook record available at https://lccn.loc.gov/2019022316

Manufactured in the United States of America
1-45001-35837-9/23/2019

CONTENTS

A **VERY** STRANGE **MYSTERY**

IN SOUTHERN AFRICA, IN PARTS OF BOTSWANA AND NAMIBIA, PEOPLE TELL OF A STRANGE HERD OF PLAINS ZEBRAS THAT GRAZE ALONG THE CHOBE (CHOH-BEE) RIVER.** Each year, during the dry season, they disappear. No one sees the herd anywhere in the area for months. Then just as mysteriously, the zebras reappear, grazing where they'd been before.

Where in the world do the zebras go? No one knew.

More than two thousand big, black-and-white zebras are in the disappearing herd, so it should be easy to spot—wherever it goes.

Long ago, such mysteries could have gone unsolved. But surprisingly, this zebra herd's vanishing act was still a mystery in the twenty-first century—an era when scientists have the tools to monitor animals large and small wherever they go. And plains zebras are big—as much as 5 feet (1.5 m) tall at the shoulder and weighing as much as 900 pounds (408 kg). Their black-and-white striped coats make them striking standouts on the landscape. How could a large herd of them disappear?

The plains zebra, also called the Burchell's or, common, zebra, is the most common and widespread type of zebra.

The position of a zebra's eyes and ears let it watch and listen for predators while getting a drink.

The Chobe River floodplains provide the zebras with a year-round water and grass supply, so it's surprising that they would leave. Zebras need to drink water nearly every day. So why does the zebra herd abandon this water supply? They leave during the dry season when many other water sources are dry. And where do they go?

LAND OF TWO SEASONS

Savannas are flat or gently rolling lands covered with grass and dotted with a few low-growing trees. They cover nearly half the African continent. Savanna ecosystems have two distinct seasons: a dry season and a wet season.

During the dry season, the savanna rarely receives more than 4 inches (10 cm) of rain. Across the savanna, the grasses turn brown. Water holes and even some streams dry up. When the water sources are dry, zebra herds and other grazing animals migrate, walking long distances to search for drinking water and plants to eat. Only the plants close to water, such as those along the Chobe River, stay green.

Look how brown and dry the Chobe River floodplain is during the dry season.

The wet season is critical for keeping the savannas thriving. During the wet season, 15 to 25 inches (38 to 64 cm) of rain falls. The rain brings the dried grasses back to life. Fresh stalks push up from the soil, and new seeds sprout and grow.

Check out how green and lush the savanna is during the wet season.

In 2012 Robin Naidoo, a research scientist with the World Wildlife Fund, decided to put together a team to solve the mystery of the disappearing zebras.

Robin had become curious about the disappearing zebras while he was working in Namibia with Elephants Without Borders. The group had been studying elephant herds that only migrated when they needed to, such as during a drought year when more water holes than usual dried up. Elephants Without Borders's goal was to learn where the herds migrated and then to recommend protecting areas of land, so these occasional migrators wouldn't be blocked by fences or highways.

Elephant herds, like this one, are mainly made up of females with their calves.

Unlike the elephants Robin had studied, the zebras disappeared every year, so they were annual migrators. Why didn't anyone know where such a huge zebra herd went?

Robin figured studying the zebra herd's migration was going to be a big job. So he arranged for his team to partner with Elephants Without Borders. They had equipment and researchers with experience studying animal migrations.

Zebras communicate with their ears. A zebra with straight-up ears is alert and feeling good. One with laid-back ears is angry. And a zebra with pushed-forward ears is frightened.

TRAVELS FOR A BETTER LIFE

Animals migrate—travel from one area to another—for a variety of reasons. Some, such as elephants and zebras, travel to avoid harsh weather conditions or to find fresh sources of water or food. Other animals, such as godwits and caribou, travel to the best location for their young to be born.

Migrating with a big group offers animals some safety. Many eyes are watching out for hungry predators. The first-time migrators can also follow the animals that have made the journey before.

Zebras are social animals. They stay close together to help one another stay alert for the predators, such as lions, that track their travels.

One of the best-known large-group migrators are wildebeests. Each year they cross the Serengeti Plains in Africa, following the rains, which fill up water holes and supply fresh grass. Antelope and zebra herds often migrate with the wildebeests to benefit from the safety of traveling in a big group.

Migrations of large numbers of animals are awesome events. The annual migrating herd of wildebeests in Africa ranks as the world's largest migration, with an estimated one million animals.

ZEBRAS ARE LEADERS

WHEREVER THEY GO, ZEBRAS ARE THE FIRST ANIMALS TO TRAVEL TO RAINY SEASON GRAZING SITES. Scientists have discovered that's because zebras can eat the coarse, dry grass left at the end of the dry season before the rainy season starts. Their bodies are able to cope with the tough, dried-up grass.

During the dry season, zebras feed on whatever plant matter is available, including shrubs and even tree bark.

Zebras have stronger upper and lower front teeth than most other grazers.

Zebras' teeth can snip off even the toughest grass stalks. They chew and swallow the grass. Then special microbes (tiny living things) inside their digestive systems are able to break down this tough plant matter. So zebras can gain nutrition from this dried-up grass when other animals can't, because their digestive systems can process it. The microbes extract even more nutrients before what's left passes out as waste.

After the rains begin and new grass is growing, zebras are already on the grazing site. They get to be the first animals to eat their fill of the new grass stalks that sprout in the rainy season. And when stalks are fresh, grass is most nutritious.

African buffaloes follow the zebras. Their front teeth are not strong enough to snip easily through tough, dry grass stalks.

Other grazers, such as African buffaloes and antelopes, are never far behind zebra herds. They push in and claim a share of the tender, new-growth grass. Having large herds of other grazers with the zebras is another reason it should have been easy to spot the disappearing zebras wherever they went. But the zebras were never spotted anywhere in the surrounding area after they left the Chobe River.

Was it possible people just hadn't searched far enough? Could it be that the zebra herd was migrating farther than anyone had ever imagined?

TRACKING DOWN **CLUES**

HOW WAS ROBIN GOING TO FIND THE DISAPPEARING ZEBRAS? Because of his work with Elephants Without Borders, Robin was already familiar with fitting animals with Global Positioning System (GPS) tracking collars. So to track the disappearing zebras and solve the mystery, he decided to catch and collar some members of the herd. He would need to do it before early December, when the zebras usually vanished. Robert Sutcliffe, a researcher with Elephants Without Borders, would try to collar some too.

The Elephants Without Borders team fits a GPS tracking collar on a sedated elephant. They have to work quickly before it wakes up.

Putting GPS tracking collars on wild zebras wouldn't be easy. Since this zebra herd was really large, lots of eyes and ears would be alert for any possible danger—such as humans approaching in a vehicle. The zebras could take off running and quickly escape. So Robin arranged for a helicopter to fly his team to the zebra herd and hired a wildlife veterinarian, Ortwin Aschenborn, to help.

As soon as the helicopter swooped low over the grazing herd, of course the zebras took off running. But the helicopter was fast enough to chase after them.

Once spooked, zebras can run as fast as 40 miles (65 km) per hour. If captured, a zebra can fight back with a strong bite and powerful kicks.

A healthy zebra is easy to spot because its short mane stands up rather than flops over.

Robin wanted to catch and collar a mare, a female zebra. Unlike stallions, or male zebras, mares are less likely to fight with one another and damage their GPS tracking collar. Robin pointed out a mare, and the helicopter homed in on that zebra. The pilot worked to separate her from the rest of the herd.

Once the zebra split away from the herd, Ortwin leaned out of the helicopter with his tranquilizer gun. He fired, hitting that zebra with a dart. Then the helicopter landed nearby. Robin and Ortwin leaped out to work on the lightly sedated zebra and attach the GPS tracking collar. They also took photos of the zebra's stripes, because each zebra's stripe pattern is unique and can be used for identification. They had to work fast: the tranquilizer wouldn't keep the female quiet very long. And without the helicopter chasing them, other members of the herd would return to defend her.

Once back in the helicopter and airborne, Robin and his team repeated the process and collared seven other females. Meanwhile, Robert Sutcliffe and his group collared three more female zebras to collect even more tracking data. This herd could not just disappear now. Each collared zebra's precise location would be recorded every five hours and transmitted by satellite to Robin's computer. Robin was excited to study the mysterious zebra herd's migration route.

Ortwin Aschenborn covered the zebra's eyes to help it stay calm while he attached the GPS tracking collar. He also took blood and tissue samples that he would bring back to the lab to test for diseases.

Before the batteries died or the collars were removed twelve to eighteen months later, each collar reported the zebra's position at least fourteen hundred times.

THE **DATA COMES IN**

WHILE HE WAITED FOR THE ZEBRAS TO START MIGRATING, ROBIN NAIDOO WENT BACK TO HIS HOME RESEARCH LAB AT THE UNIVERSITY OF BRITISH COLUMBIA IN VANCOUVER, CANADA. There, he studied the GPS data as it came in from the collared female zebras. He used a satellite image showing the Chobe River, plus an area a little to the south as a map. On that map, he made different colored dots to record the locations of each collared zebra. He connected those dots daily with colored lines matching the dots as he began to track each female's path—and with them the zebra herd's migration route.

Here is a close-up look at one GPS tracking collar.

At first, the zebras didn't seem to be traveling very far. So over the winter holiday, Robin didn't bother to go to his lab and update the zebra's progress for a couple of weeks. But when he went back to work at the beginning of 2013, he got a *big* surprise.

The most current recorded location for each of the collared zebras was far beyond his satellite image map. Robin said, "How far the zebras had gone was absolutely amazing! And it was as if the zebras had compasses because they were making a beeline due south."

Robin knew zebras were capable of extreme long-distance migrations. Five years earlier, in 2008, Hattie Bartlam-Brooks had reported on a zebra herd setting the record for Africa's longest overland large mammal migration.

Red oat grass is a favorite food of plains zebras. It can grow to be more than 3 feet (0.9 m) tall.

Hattie is a researcher who studies the ways animals adapt to thrive where they live. She wanted to learn how the removal of farm fences in 2004 had affected a zebra herd whose migration had been blocked. The herd had completely stopped migrating because trekking around the fences meant having to go too far from any reliable source of drinking water.

That zebra herd hadn't migrated for thirty-six years. And since a zebra's average life span is only twelve years, no living members of the herd could have remembered migrating.

Zebras often walk in a line as they migrate from the Okavango River delta.

When the fences were removed to allow animals to move freely and find water, the herd started migrating again. Hattie wanted to learn where they were going. To do that, she fitted eight female zebras in the herd with GPS tracking collars. To her surprise, with the fences gone, the herd had not only resumed migrating. They followed what had, historically, been their herd's migration route. Maybe the route was part of the zebras' instinct—they didn't have to learn where to go because they

Hattie's research also showed that those migrating zebras covered almost 155 miles (250 km), following a meandering path from the Okavango (oh-kuh-VAHN-goh) River delta to the Makgadikgadi (ma-KAHD-ee-KAHD-ee) Pans National Park. With a matching return trip, that zebra herd set a record for Africa's longest overland large mammal migration.

Excited about the possibility of discovering a new record long-distance migration, Robin Naidoo continued to track the collared zebras, watching as they traveled farther and farther south.

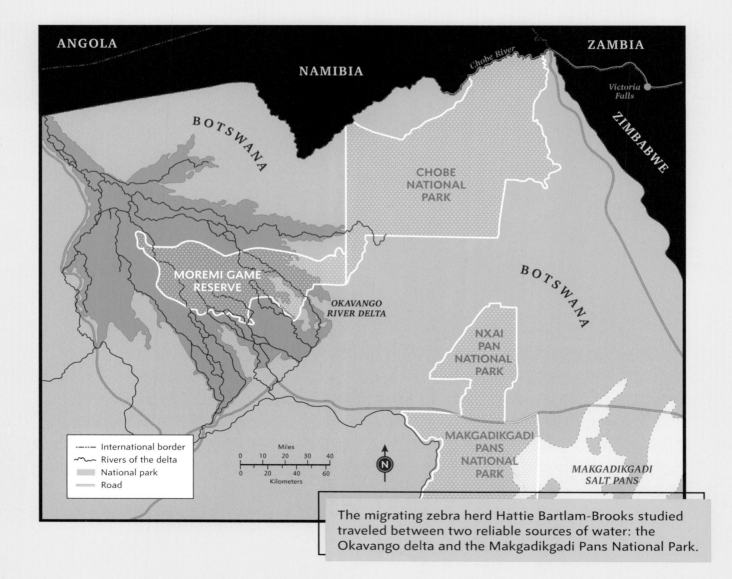

The migrating zebra herd Hattie Bartlam-Brooks studied traveled between two reliable sources of water: the Okavango delta and the Makgadikgadi Pans National Park.

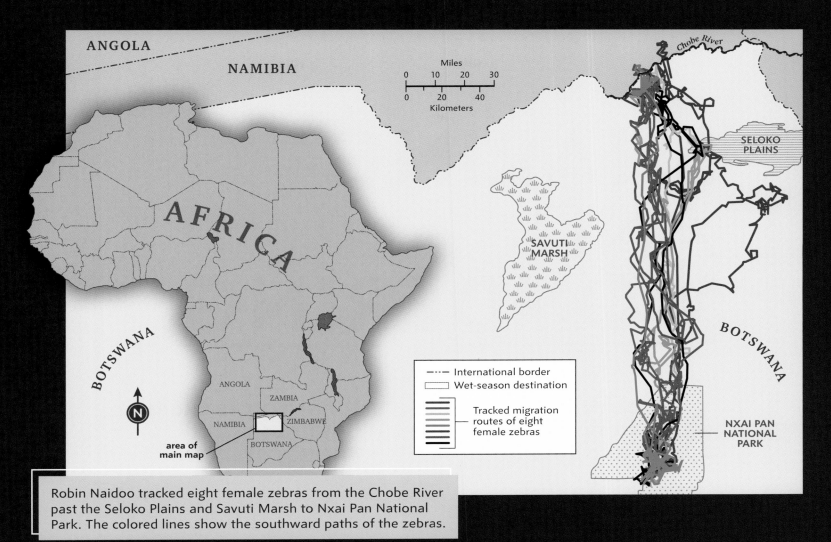

Robin Naidoo tracked eight female zebras from the Chobe River past the Seloko Plains and Savuti Marsh to Nxai Pan National Park. The colored lines show the southward paths of the zebras.

Before they stopped, the mysterious zebra herd trekked all the way to Nxai (N-eye) Pan National Park in Botswana—a little more than 155 miles (250 km). So they traveled a bit farther than Hattie's record-holding zebra migration. And they hadn't meandered—they'd gone straight to their destination.

The mystery of where the disappearing zebras went was solved. And the herd had set a brand-new record for Africa's longest overland large mammal migration.

SHARING AND WONDERING

MONTHS LATER, ON ITS RETURN TRIP TO THE CHOBE RIVER FLOODPLAINS, THE MYSTERIOUS ZEBRA HERD MEANDERED BACK TO WHERE IT STARTED. That meant the herd's total migration was 593 miles (955 km). Amazingly, that made the total migration more than three times farther than the total travels of Hattie's record-setting herd.

It was time for Robin and his team to share what they'd discovered and get feedback from other migration researchers.

In 2013 they worked with their partners at Elephants Without Borders to write a report about their research. It included what they'd studied, where they'd worked, and how they'd collected data, or scientific information. Then it described what they'd found. Robin gave this report to a number of other scientists who were studying zebra migrations. These experts reviewed the work—a process called peer review. The experts gave Robin a list of questions they felt the report needed to explain more fully. Robin, his team, and their partners at Elephants Without Borders worked together to make the revisions. In 2014 Cambridge University Press's scientific journal *Oryx* accepted and published the report.

But this wasn't the end of the detective work for Robin. While working on the report revisions, he and his team figured out something else they needed to investigate about the mysterious herd's migration.

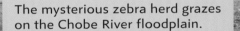

The mysterious zebra herd grazes on the Chobe River floodplain.

THE **REST** OF THE **MYSTERY**

ROBIN KNEW THAT WATER AND NEW GRASS WERE AVAILABLE CLOSER TO THE CHOBE RIVER THAN THE NXAI PAN. So why did the zebras head straight to the Nxai Pan? Robin needed to investigate.

A side benefit of the zebras migrating away from the Chobe River is it gives the floodplains a chance to recover from being trampled by thousands of hooves. The grasses have the chance to grow back.

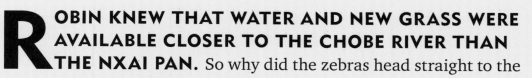

To find out, during 2014 and 2015, Robin and his team tracked thirty zebras. One of those zebras—nicknamed Janet—was still wearing her old, numbered collar from 2012. So she'd been part of the original tracking study. This time, as Robin followed Janet's migration route again, he made an amazing discovery: "That zebra followed nearly the same route to and from the Nxai Pan in 2015 as she did in 2012. And she made stops at almost exactly the same times during each migration."

Robert added, "The zebra[s] probably go straight to the Nxai Pan because they can." The direct route was across a huge area of protected land free of any barrier fences.

Robin Naidoo adjusts the GPS collar on one of the new test zebras.

Robin and his team concluded that the zebra herd took this direct route because many of the mares are about ready to give birth, and they will need to nurse (provide milk for) their young. Nursing requires a lot of energy, so mares with foals need the highest-quality food they can find. Robert explained, "We've discovered that the soils at the Nxai Pan have just the right mineral content to produce very nutritious grass. And the first new sprouts of the wet season are extra nutritious. That's very important for nursing mares."

On the zebras' return trip to the Chobe River, the rainy season is just ending, so there's plenty to eat and all the water holes are full.

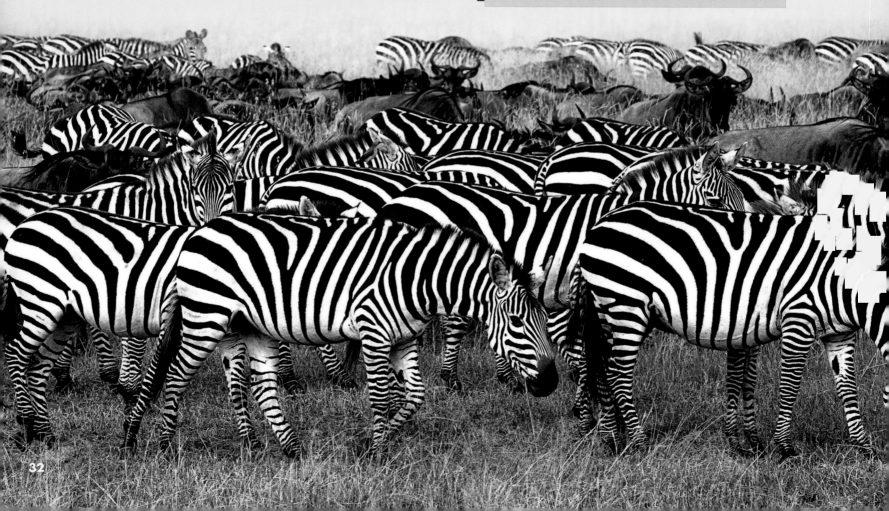

A HERD OF FAMILIES

A herd of plains zebras is made up of a number of family groups. Each has a stallion and at least one mare with her foal. A family group may include several mares with foals.

Each mare usually has only one foal at a time, giving birth after the baby has developed inside her body for twelve to thirteen months. Within minutes of its birth, a foal can stand and walk. In just an hour, it is strong enough to travel with its family. A mare nurses her foal for as long as sixteen months, but the foal also starts grazing when it's barely a week old. In order to get the microbes necessary to digest grass, it eats some adult dung (solid waste) too.

At birth a zebra foal weighs 55 to 88 pounds (25 to 40 kg), and it is about 33 inches (84 cm) tall at the shoulder. It quickly grows bigger.

Robin was glad to solve this additional mystery about the disappearing zebra herd's migration. But what he'd learned alarmed him. Africa's environment is slowly heating up, causing the wet season to start later. If the migration launch is triggered by the pregnant females' rush to reach the Nxai Pan to give birth, a delay in the rains could mean water holes along their route are still dry. If the zebras somehow sense when the rains are coming and that triggers the migration, they might delay heading for the Nxai Pan. Then foals could be born before the migration starts or along the way. The long trek might be too much for these young animals—weakened, they'd be easy prey for predators.

One of the reasons for the zebra herd's slower return trip was that many mares were accompanied by foals.

The effects of climate change can't be completely altered, but finding out that the zebra herd stayed with the same migration route made it possible to help them. Conservation groups based in Namibia and Botswana now know which land needs to remain free of fences. They also know which water holes need wells to ensure the migrating animals have water at key stops.

Thanks to the hard work and research of Robin Naidoo and his team, people in parts of Namibia and Botswana still tell the story of one very special herd of plains zebra, but they're no longer mysterious—they're awesome, record-setting migrators.

And it's a story that doesn't have an ending—**IT HAS A FUTURE!**

Although zebras can go as long as five days without water, they're healthier if they drink water daily.

AUTHOR'S NOTE

I couldn't resist digging into the mystery of Africa's disappearing zebra herd. I mean, two thousand big, black-and-white zebras are grazing along a river one day, gone the next, and not spotted anywhere in the area until they show up again months later. Fascinating! And nobody had a clue where the zebras went, though they'd been pulling this disappearing act for as long as people in the area could remember. Plus the plot thickens, because it's not as if the herd needs to find water. The zebras leave the Chobe River—a year-round, dependable water supply—ahead of Africa's rainy season starting. *WOW—what a cool mystery!*

Tracking down who worked on solving this scientific mystery and what they discovered also gave me a chance to be a detective. I followed leads to locate and contact the scientists investigating this case. I was able to learn how they did it and what they learned firsthand. So don't miss the scientists' quotes I've shared in the story. These provide insights into the hard work and creative thinking that went into solving the migration mystery. That way, you'll be able to join me in the fun of being an investigative reporter. Finding out the solution to the mystery is cool—getting to know the amazing scientist-detectives is a bonus!

PLAINS ZEBRA FAST FACTS

- In a National Geographic Society study, researchers discovered tiny, swirling air currents over a zebra's body. These air currents are created because the black areas soak up more heat than the white areas. The temperature difference is just enough to generate tiny breezes.

- Under their black-and-white coats, zebras have black skin.

- Plains zebra foals often have brown stripes at first. They start to get their adult coloring when they're just four months old.

- When fleeing from a predator, zebras usually run in a zigzag pattern, making them hard to run down.

- Zebras have single hooves like their cousins, horses and donkeys. Antelope and deer have split hooves.

- Zebras spend so much time crushing and grinding their food with their back molars that those teeth wear down. Luckily, their molars keep growing their whole lives, so zebras can keep eating.

- A group of zebras is a dazzle, or a zeal.

Zebra family members use their lips and teeth to nibble on one another's necks, shoulders, and backs. This helps them bond.

GLOSSARY

adapt: to make changes in a species, over generations, that help the individuals in that species become better able to survive in their environment

annual: something that happens every year, often at the same time of year

ecosystem: an interconnected community of plants and animals

foal: a young zebra

habitat: an animal's home area that supplies the food, water, and shelter it needs to live plus the place it can raise its young

instinct: a natural ability to do something that doesn't have to be learned

mammal: an animal that nourishes its young with milk and that has hair

mare: a female zebra

microbe: tiny living thing

migrate: to move from one part of its habitat to another, usually seasonally

nurse: a young animal drinking milk from its mother's body, or the mother producing milk for her young

predator: an animal that hunts prey and eats what it catches

prey: an animal a predator catches to eat

savanna: a grassy plain with few trees

sedated: being calmer and more relaxed as an effect of a tranquilizer (or as an effect of a drug)

stallion: a male zebra

tranquilizer: a drug used to calm

SOURCE NOTES

23   Robin Naidoo, telephone interview with author, August 10, 2018.

31   Naidoo.

31   Robert Sutcliffe, telephone interview with author, August 7, 2018.

32   Sutcliffe.

FIND OUT MORE

Check out these books and websites to discover even more about zebras and their migration:

Carney, Elizabeth. *Great Migrations: Whales, Wildebeests, Butterflies, Elephants and Other Amazing Animals on the Move.* Washington, DC: National Geographic Kids, 2010. Compare zebra migrations to the migrations of other animals.

Gregory, Josh. *African Savanna.* North Mankato, MN: Cherry Lake, 2016. Explore the African savanna where the plains zebra herds live. Discover what there is about this habitat that causes the zebras to migrate.

Markle, Sandra. *Zebras.* Minneapolis: Lerner Publications, 2007. Follow one zebra family and their herd as they slowly migrate to find food, avoid predators, and have a young foal grow up on the African plains.

National Geographic Kids: Zebra Facts!
https://www.natgeokids.com/nz/discover/animals/general-animals/zebra-facts/
Cool facts about the three kinds of zebras: plains zebras, Grevy's zebras, and mountain zebras.

"Zebras' Migration Longer Than Any Other in Africa"
https://www.youtube.com/watch?v=n0vrC5tFML4
Watch a movie about the plains zebra's record-breaking long-distance migration.

INDEX

PHOTO ACKNOWLEDGMENTS